Ready·Set·Learn

Reading Comprehension

3

180+ Stickers Inside

Editor in Chief
Ina Massler Levin, M.A.

Editor
Eric Migliaccio

Contributing Editor
Sarah Smith

Creative Director
Karen J. Goldfluss, M.S. Ed.

Cover Design
Tony Carrillo / Marilyn Goldberg

Teacher Created Resources, Inc.
6421 Industry Way
Westminster, CA 92683
www.teachercreated.com

ISBN: 978-1-4206-5929-0

© 2008 Teacher Created Resources, Inc.
Made in U.S.A.

Teacher Created Resources

SO-DZF-367

This book belongs to

_____

Ready·Set·Learn

Get Ready to Learn!

Get ready, get set, and go! Boost your child's learning with this exciting series of books. Geared to help children practice and master many needed skills, the *Ready·Set·Learn* books are bursting with 64 pages of learning fun. Use these books for . . .

 enrichment   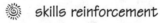 skills reinforcement   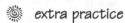 extra practice

With their smaller size, the *Ready·Set·Learn* books fit easily in children's hands, backpacks, and book bags. All your child needs to get started are pencils, crayons, and colored pencils.

A full sheet of colorful stickers is included. Use these stickers for . . .

☀ decorating pages

☀ rewarding outstanding effort

☀ keeping track of completed pages

Celebrate your child's progress by using these stickers on the reward chart located on the inside cover. The blue-ribbon sticker fits perfectly on the certificate on page 64.

With *Ready·Set·Learn* and a little encouragement, your child will be on the fast track to learning fun!

Weird Weather

Weather does weird things. Air currents can raise the temperature of a city 100 degrees in just one day. Wind can lift heavy objects into the air. Sudden rainstorms can flood huge areas. Once in a while even stranger things happen.

For example, sometimes snow is pink. Snow forms in clouds high in the atmosphere. A strong wind may pick up red dirt on the ground. The dirt rises high into the air and mixes with the snow. When the snow falls to the ground, the snow looks dark pink. Pink snow is rare. Although people rarely see it, it does happen.

Even stranger things fall from the sky. One time, in France, it rained toads! It was a rainy day in a small town near Paris. The rain falling on the people's raincoats and umbrellas seemed normal. Suddenly, big, heavy toads started dropping out of the sky. The toads smashed windows. They bounced off people's heads. The people were very scared. It was a real mystery.

How can toads fall from the sky? Scientists have a simple explanation. They think waterspouts cause it. Waterspouts are tornadoes that form over lakes or oceans. Sometimes, a waterspout's strong wind lifts heavy objects into the air. The wind can even lift toads. A waterspout loses power when it moves over  land. When this happens, whatever it lifted from the water falls to the ground.

Weather is hard to predict. When strange things happen, they are difficult to explain. Remember this the next time you listen to a weather report. Don't be scared if the report says, "Watch out for falling toads in the morning, with a chance of pink snow by late afternoon!"

Weird Weather (cont.)

Directions: Read the story and circle the correct answer.

1. Why did toads fall from the sky?
   a. Waterspouts lifted them into the air.
   b. They fell from the clouds.
   c. Scientists do not know why.
   d. They fell out of airplanes.

2. Sudden rainstorms can . . .
   a. flood huge areas.
   b. pick up red dirt from the ground.
   c. smash windows.
   d. lift heavy objects into the air.

3. The first paragraph tells you . . .
   a. that weather is sometimes strange.
   b. that pink snow is rare.
   c. what waterspouts are.
   d. how toads can fall from the sky.

4. You can tell that the word "rare" means . . .
   a. uncommon.   c. sudden.
   b. mysterious.   d. pink.

5. What is the main idea of this passage?
   a. Air currents can raise temperatures.
   b. Snow forms in clouds high in the atmosphere.
   c. Weather can be unpredictable and weird.
   d. Toads are big and heavy.

Habitat for Humanity

Thirty years ago, Linda and Millard Fuller started Habitat for Humanity. This program builds houses for families that need them. The money that the family is able to pay for the needed house goes back to Habitat for Humanity. That money is then used to help build more houses. A lot of the money for the houses comes from donations. Many people also donate their time to help build the houses. This means they do not get paid. They are called volunteers.

Many of the volunteers are people who build houses for a living. Some have no building experience but still want to help. The people who are going to move into one of the houses also help build it. They work side by side with the volunteers. The frame of the house has to be built. The roof has to be put on. The walls have to be painted. Everyone puts in a lot of time hammering, painting, sawing, and gluing until the job is done.

Habitat for Humanity has built more than 200,000 houses around the world. They have helped to make life better for many people, one house at time.

Directions: Circle the letter next to the correct answer.

1. Who started Habitat for Humanity?
   a. Linda and Fuller Millard
   b. Fuller and Linda Millard
   c. Linda and Millard Fuller
   d. President and Mrs. Gerald Ford

2. According to the passage, *volunteers* are people who . . .
   a. know how to build houses.
   b. don't like to paint.
   c. families that live in houses.
   d. don't get paid.

3. How many houses have Habitat for Humanity built?
   a. over 200,000
   b. 200
   c. more than 1,000,000
   d. 500

4. We can best describe Millard and Linda as . . .
   a. people who love to save their money.
   b. people who care about helping others.
   c. people who love to buy fancy things.
   d. people who live in a big house.

Classifying Animals

Did you know that there are over 1,000,000 different species, or types, of animals? With so many species, scientists have to find a way to sort them into groups. Two of the main groups are vertebrates and invertebrates.

Vertebrates are animals that have a backbone. Humans are in this group. Also in this group are whales, monkeys, birds, and frogs. Just about any pet you have in your home is a vertebrate. Dogs, cats, goldfish, hamsters, and snakes are vertebrates.

Invertebrates have no backbone. Many of them live in the ocean. Clams, jellyfish, squids, and octopuses are invertebrates. Those that live on land are spiders, worms, and insects.

Scientists are finding new species of animals every day. Every one of them can be put into one of these two groups.

Directions: Circle the letter next to the correct answer.

1. What are two ways animals are classified or sorted?
   - a. land and water animals
   - b. mammals and jellyfish
   - c. invertebrates and vertebrates
   - d. color and shape

2. Based on the passage, which is the best definition of invertebrates?
   - a. animals that have several backbones
   - b. animals that have one backbone
   - c. animals that have no backbone
   - d. animals that prefer to swim in the ocean

3. Human beings are in the category of . . .
   - a. invertebrates.
   - b. vertebrates.
   - c. neither of these.
   - d. both of these.

4. Which of the animals below would fit into the category of invertebrates?
   - a. giraffe
   - b. bird
   - c. squid
   - d. pig

The Wood Carver

Ever since Greg was a toddler, he had watched his grandfather carve the small wooden figures. Greg was fascinated with the quickness of his grandfather's fingers as he switched the carving knife from one hand to the other, breathing life into what was once a lifeless piece of wood. Greg often wished that he could create wonderful little wooden figurines, as his grandfather did.

One day, Greg's grandfather called the boy into the workshop. "Today is the day that you begin to learn the lost art of carving." Greg couldn't believe his ears as he pulled up a small stool next to his grandfather's workbench. The sharp smell of the wood filled his nose, and he moved in closely to where his grandfather was working. Greg's head was soon reeling with the names of the different tools his grandfather used to create the wooden treasures.

After the introduction to the tools was complete, Greg picked up a piece of wood to make his first attempt at carving. He loved the feel of the rough wood biting into his fingers. He worked for hours that day, trying to duplicate his grandfather's skill. Although his small, wooden figurine was far from perfect, both Greg and his grandfather were quite proud of the work Greg had done. "This piece will occupy a place of honor on my shelf," Greg's grandfather told him. Greg's eyes shone with joy. He knew that it would take many years to become as skillful as his grandfather, but Greg was going to enjoy every minute of it!

8

The Wood Carver *(cont.)*

Directions: Read the story and circle the correct answer.

1. How did Greg feel when he watched his grandfather carve wood?
   a. worried that his grandfather would cut himself
   b. frustrated that he couldn't carve like his grandfather
   c. angry that his grandfather wouldn't teach him how to carve
   d. amazed by his grandfather's skill

2. What will Greg probably do now that he's had his first lesson?
   a. keep working on it to get better
   b. give up because he isn't as good as his grandfather
   c. throw out his first figurine
   d. chop down a tree in order to get some wood

3. Why did Greg's grandfather put Greg's wooden figure on the shelf?
   a. Greg's grandfather knew it was not a good piece of work.
   b. Greg's grandfather was proud of Greg's first wood carving.
   c. It was the best wood carving Greg's grandfather had ever seen.
   d. That is where Greg's grandfather always put the wooden figures.

4. Why did Greg's grandfather call wood carving a "lost art"?
   a. Not many people carve wood by hand anymore.
   b. Carving wood was done only by lost people.
   c. No one knows how to carve wood.
   d. There are no books about carving wood.

5. What does it mean to "breathe life into" a piece of wood?
   a. Greg's grandfather would make hollow wood pieces like whistles.
   b. Greg's grandfather could make a real-looking figure out of a piece of wood.
   c. Greg's grandfather always blew on the wood before he carved it.
   d. Carving wood could turn a dead piece of wood into a living one.

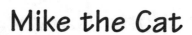

Mike the Cat

Mike the cat was an ordinary cat. He had two ears, four paws, and a short, stubby tail. Wait a minute! A short, stubby tail? All the other cats that Mike had seen had long tails. Some tails were fluffy and some were not—but they were all long. Mike decided that his short tail would never do. He had to get a long tail! But how?

Mike traveled far and wide, trying to find a long tail. Along the way, he spoke with many cats that had long tails. "My, what an unusual cat you are!" they would say. "We have never seen a cat with a short, stubby tail." The cats would gather around Mike, asking all sorts of questions about what it was like to have a short tail. Mike often found himself talking into the wee hours of the morning, telling stories of how he could sleep in front of warm fireplaces, never having to worry whether someone was going to step on his tail. Or about the times that he slipped out the back door and spent sunny afternoons chasing squirrels, when the slamming door would have caught other cats by the tail. It wasn't long before Mike became something of a celebrity! Other cats came to him to hear his amazing stories.

Soon, Mike forgot that he had left home in order to find a long tail! Maybe being a cat with a short, stubby tail wasn't so bad. Because of his unique quality, Mike had made many friends. "I guess being one-of-a-kind is not so bad after all," Mike thought. "I think I'll keep my short, stubby tail."

Mike the Cat (cont.)

Directions: Read the story and circle the correct answer.

1. Why did Mike decide that his short, stubby tail wasn't so bad?
   a. He was tired from traveling far and wide.
   b. He had made new friends because of his strange tail.
   c. He saw how other cats had short tails, too.
   d. He didn't like the longer tails of the other cats.

2. What is the main point of this story?
   a. Being different is not so bad after all.
   b. The only way to have friends is to be different.
   c. No one should be teased for being different.
   d. It is important to be like everyone else.

3. What does it mean that Mike became "something of a celebrity"?
   a. Mike became popular because of his stories about his unusual tail.
   b. Mike starred in cat food commercials.
   c. Mike stood out because of his long, fluffy tail.
   d. Mike wanted to be the most popular of all cats.

4. What is Mike likely to do next?
   a. find out how he can grow a longer tail
   b. find another way to be unique
   c. encourage the other cats to have short tails
   d. be happy with his short, stubby tail

5. Why did the other cats gather around Mike?
   a. to ask him questions about his tail
   b. to take pictures of mike's tail
   c. to find out how they could have a tail like his
   d. to ask him why his tail was long and fluffy

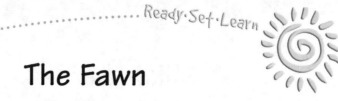

The Fawn

Sara and her father planned a hike up a mountain trail near their home. The trail they chose began at the foot of the mountain and led all the way to the top. Sara had packed lunches earlier that morning. Her father filled their backpacks with other supplies, and they were off!

As they started up the trail, Sara's father pointed out many different plants that lined the trail. He showed Sara the difference between the leaves of an aspen tree and the needles of a spruce tree. Sara was glad that her father knew so much! She always learned something whenever they went on a hike.

"Look over there," Sara whispered suddenly. They had just turned a corner on the mountain trail. Lying in the grass next to the trail was a small baby deer, or fawn. It looked at them with wide eyes, but it did not move.

"Where is its mother?" Sara wondered aloud. "Do you think we should stay here and watch it?"

"That's a good idea," answered her dad. "We must not go any closer, though." As they sat down and unpacked their lunch, Sara asked her dad why they couldn't go any closer to the fawn. He explained that sometimes if the mother smelled humans too close to her baby, she would be too afraid to come back. Sara and her father agreed that they would wait for the mother to come back, but that they would not get too close to the fawn.

Soon a larger deer walked slowly up to the fawn nestled in the grass. After a few quick sniffs and a cautious glance at Sara and her father, mother and baby ran quickly down the trail.

Sara and her father packed up their supplies and continued up the mountain. They knew that the fawn was now safe.

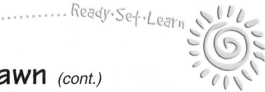

The Fawn *(cont.)*

Directions: Read the story and circle the correct answer.

1. How does Sara's dad probably feel about the fawn?
    a. He wants to ignore it.
    b. He cares about its survival.
    c. He doesn't want to help it.
    d. He wishes he could be one.

2. What is the main idea of this story?
    a. There is a hiking trail near Sara's house.
    b. Sara's dad teaches her about trees and plants.
    c. A mother deer returns for her fawn.
    d. Sara learns a lesson from her dad while on a hike.

3. What is a good word to describe Sara's dad?
    a. wise
    b. boring
    c. funny
    d. strict

4. After this experience, what would Sara probably do if she were by herself and saw another fawn?
    a. run up to it
    b. watch it from a distance
    c. feed it
    d. teach it about trees

5. How will Sara's dad probably feel about her after the hike is over?
    a. proud
    b. angry
    c. puzzled
    d. sad

Cheetahs Are Fast Cats

Cheetahs are fast cats. They can outrun any other land animal on Earth. They can go from standing still to running 45 miles per hour in just 2.5 seconds. And they can keep up this pace for more than three miles! Their top speed is 70 miles per hour. But they can only go that fast for 300 yards. Cheetahs have a flexible spine that acts as a spring for their back legs. This gives the big cat extra distance between each step. While running, just one foot touches the ground at a time.

The name cheetah means "spotted one." Cheetahs have spots over nearly their whole bodies. Just their white necks and bellies have none. Not only are these big cats beautiful, they will not attack humans. Royalty in ancient cultures often kept them as pets. Paintings show them living with people 5,000 years ago. Although they are easy to tame, today it is against the law to keep one as a pet.

Cheetahs live on grassy plains. They like to lie on tree branches and watch for prey. They do this in the early morning and late afternoon. They hunt rabbits or small antelope.

Each female gives birth to two to eight cubs. But nine out of every 10 cubs die by the age of three months. Lions and hyenas eat them. So, while they are babies, their mother moves them to a new hiding spot each day. By the time they are five months old, the cubs can outrun predators. Babies stay with their mothers for up to two years before finding their own territory.

At one point long ago, nearly all cheetahs died out. Just a few were left to breed. As a result, all cheetahs have similar genes. Now these big cats are dying out again. In 1900 there were 100,000 in Africa and India. Today there are less than 13,000 in Africa. None live in India. Why? People have built homes and farms. This has cut down on the cheetah's hunting grounds. And even though people want to breed them, it hasn't worked well. Cheetahs in zoos rarely breed. Most often if a zoo has a cheetah, it came from the wild.

Cheetahs Are Fast Cats (cont.)

1. For a short distance a cheetah can run . . .
    a. 45 miles per hour.
    b. 70 miles per hour.
    c. 300 miles per hour.

2. Cheetahs hunt . . .
    a. in the afternoon.
    b. just after sunset.
    c. after it gets completely dark.

3. Since female cheetahs have multiple cubs, why are there so few adult cheetahs?
    a. People steal cheetah babies from the wild to raise as pets.
    b. The mother cheetah will only take care of two cubs no matter how many she has.
    c. Hyenas and lions eat most of the cheetah babies.

4. Cheetahs used to live on two continents. What are their names? On which continent do they still live?

_____

_____

_____

_____

5. Is it good that a law now prevents cheetahs from being pets? Why or why not?

_____

_____

_____

_____

Earthquakes

The Earth's surface is called the crust. The crust is made up of about 30 huge plates. Most plates hold some land and some ocean floor. They float on a layer called the mantle. Because the plates drift, the continents are always moving. The continents move about four inches each year. This means that in about 20 million years Africa will join with Europe.

When the plates move, they change the Earth's features. Some plates have run into each other. One pushed up over the top of the other. This made mountains. Each huge plate has edges. These edges are called fault lines. They often meet under the ocean. In some places they meet on land. Earthquakes happen along these lines. A major fault line reaches from California through Alaska. Another goes from the Rocky Mountains down into Mexico.

An earthquake happens when the Earth's plates shift along a fault. Earthquakes make the ground shake—sometimes up to 1,000 miles away. Many earthquakes happen each day. But people only feel the strong ones. A strong earthquake can really change the surface of the Earth. It can leave big cracks in the ground. Sometimes it causes landslides. In a landslide, parts of hills fall into the valley. The quake can also leave new ridges many miles long.

Earthquakes (cont.)

Directions: Fill in the bubble next to the best answer. You may look back at the story.

1. Where are fault lines?
   - ⓐ They are on land and under the sea.
   - ⓑ They are only on land.
   - ⓒ They are only under the sea.
   - ⓓ They are under rivers.

2. What happens first?
   - ⓐ Parts of the hill end up in the valley.
   - ⓑ The ground shakes.
   - ⓒ One of the Earth's plates moves.
   - ⓓ There is a landslide.

3. Which does not happen during an earthquake?
   - ⓐ The ground cracks.   ⓒ Buildings fall down.
   - ⓑ There is a big forest fire.   ⓓ New hills are formed.

4. The word that means the same as *shift* is
   - ⓐ stop.   ⓒ twist.
   - ⓑ move.   ⓓ glide.

5. Under the ocean . . .
   - ⓐ there are no fault lines.
   - ⓑ earthquakes can't happen because of the weight of the water.
   - ⓒ earthquakes do happen but the ocean floor does not change.
   - ⓓ earthquakes happen along fault lines.

6. Picture how an area looks after an earthquake. Which would you most likely see?
   - ⓐ a forest fire with lots of smoke
   - ⓑ a snowstorm making cars skid
   - ⓒ lava flowing in the street
   - ⓓ a big crack down the middle of a road

Animal Adaptations

Animals can change the way they act to make it easier to live in their environments. This change is called adaptation. An adaptation may be learned. If an animal learns a new skill that keeps it alive, it will live longer than other animals like it. It will have more babies. These babies will be taught that skill by their parents.

During heavy rains in South America, big pieces of land floated down the rivers. The land carried animals like iguanas (lizards). They drifted right out to sea. After some time the pieces collided with a group of islands. They are called the Galapagos Islands.

The iguanas that had drifted to the islands had to adapt to their new environment. Iguanas eat green plants. But they could not find enough to eat on land. They got very hungry. Then they saw that there were lots of green plants below the water. Some of the iguanas jumped into the water. They swam to the bottom. They ate the green plants. Only the iguanas that learned to swim got enough to eat. So those that didn't learn to swim died. Today, all of the iguanas living there can swim. It is the only place in the world with iguanas that know how to swim. It is the only place where they had to learn to swim in order to stay alive.

18

Animal Adaptations (cont.)

Directions: Fill in the bubble next to the best answer. You may look back at the story.

1. Where did the plants and animals in the Galapagos Islands come from?
   - ⓐ South America
   - ⓑ North America
   - ⓒ Central America
   - ⓓ Australia

2. What happened first?
   - ⓐ The iguanas couldn't find enough to eat.
   - ⓑ The pieces of land came to an island group.
   - ⓒ Rain washed pieces of land into the sea.
   - ⓓ The iguanas learned how to swim.

3. What makes Galapagos iguanas different from all other iguanas?
   - ⓐ They do not eat green plants.
   - ⓑ They eat green plants.
   - ⓒ They know how to swim.
   - ⓓ They do not know how to swim.

4. The word *collided* means the same thing as . . .
   - ⓐ sunk.　　ⓑ went around.　　ⓒ left.　　ⓓ ran into.

5. A pet bunny runs away and can't find her way back home. What must she do to survive?
   - ⓐ find a mate
   - ⓑ find food and water
   - ⓒ find shelter
   - ⓓ find food, water, and shelter

6. Picture the chunks of land floating to the Galapagos Islands. Besides the iguanas, what else do you see carried on the land?
   - ⓐ a river　　ⓑ plants　　ⓒ a mountain　　ⓓ fish

Railroads

Did you know that the idea for trains started in Germany? In 1550, some roads in Germany had wooden rails. They ran along the road. They were called "wagon ways." These roads were used for wagons pulled by horses. They were easier than traveling on dirt roads.

1n 1776, metal rails were made. The rails were made of iron. They were called "tramways." They were very popular. They went all over Europe. A man named William Jesse had an idea. He made wheels with a groove, or cut-out edge. These wheels helped the wagons move faster on the iron rails. The wagons were still pulled by horses.

The steam engine came next. A man named Richard Trevithick wanted to move people and things from place to place without using animals. He made an advanced steam engine. It could carry 10 tons of iron, 70 men, and five wagons for 9 miles in two hours.

A man named John Stevens put all of these ideas together. He is called the "father of the American railroad." He showed how steam trains would work. He got the first charter railroad.

Each new idea has made traveling easier and faster.

Directions: Circle the letter next to the correct answer.

1. Who was called the "father of the American railroad"?
   a. Richard Trevithick   c. Orlando Bloom
   b. William Jesse   d. John Stevens

2. Which words best describe the "wagon ways"?
   a. wooden rails   c. steam engines
   b. iron rails   d. fire wagons

3. Which word is an antonym for the word *pulled*?
   a. snatched   b. grabbed   c. pushed   d. yanked

4. Which statement is NOT true about the history of the railroads?
   a. The idea for trains began in Germany.
   b. Today trains run very slowly and are pulled by horses.
   c. "Tramways" had rails made of iron.
   d. Today trains run much faster and easier than in the past.

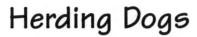

Herding Dogs

Did you know that herding dogs come in many shapes and sizes? Some are tall. Some are short. Some are lean, and some are stocky. The shortest herding dogs are Welsh corgis. These little dogs were bred to herd cattle. Their short legs move quickly when they run around the herd, and their short, little bodies can avoid a kick from an angry cow.

Most herding dogs are medium-sized. The border collie is famous for its intelligence. These dogs are active and always moving. They look for cues from the shepherd, and they work as a team. Border collies could almost work alone. They know what to do if a sheep strays.

Large dogs, like German shepherds and Belgian sheepdogs, work many jobs. They can herd, but more often they work with police, guide the blind, or provide protection to families.

Herding dogs are also trained for search and rescue work. Often, during a disaster you will see teams of dogs working to find missing people.

Today, most dogs don't work in the jobs they were bred to do. People love them as pets.

Directions: Circle the letter next to the correct answer.

1. Which breed is the shortest herding dog?
   a. Shetland sheepdog   b. Welsh corgi   c. puli   d. collie

2. The border collie is a good pet for someone who . . .
   a. likes to lounge on the couch all evening.
   b. doesn't have a backyard.
   c. is active and enjoys taking the dog on long walks.
   d. worries about dog hair on the sofa.

3. How has the job of the herding dog changed over the years?
   a. All are trained as search and rescue dogs.
   b. Some owners take their dogs to the beach.
   c. Some have become pets and are no longer trained to perform traditional jobs.
   d. They make great babysitters.

Fossils

Long ago an animal died. It fell to the ground. Mud covered it. Over time, more mud pressed down on it. After a very long time, its bones changed into rock. This rock is called a fossil.

Many scientists look for fossils. They find them in very old rocks. Some fossils are millions of years old. Many of the fossil animals and plants have died off. The only way we know about them is by their fossils. Dinosaurs did not live at the same time as humans. There are no drawings of them on cave walls. So in 1822, when the first dinosaur fossil was found, people were amazed.

People are always digging for fossils. They find them all over the world. Fossils have even been found in Antarctica. And new kinds of dinosaurs are still being discovered. The people who dig for dinosaur bones can learn a lot about a dinosaur from its fossil. They can look at the teeth and tell whether the dinosaur ate plants or meat. If it had flat teeth, it ate plants. If it had pointed teeth, it ate other animals. But fossils cannot tell us everything we'd like to know. For example, we are not sure that dinosaurs were reptiles. We are not sure if they all laid eggs or if some had live babies. And because only their bones are left, we may never know what colors the dinosaurs were.

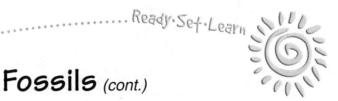

Fossils *(cont.)*

Directions: Fill in the bubble next to the best answer. You may look back at the story.

1. A dinosaur fossil with flat teeth lets you know that . . .
   - ⓐ the dinosaur laid eggs.
   - ⓑ the dinosaur weighed more than most.
   - ⓒ the dinosaur ate plants.
   - ⓓ the dinosaur ate other animals.

2. What happened first?
   - ⓐ An animal died long ago.
   - ⓑ The mud and bones turned into a fossil.
   - ⓒ Mud covered the body.
   - ⓓ A scientist dug up the fossil.

3. What do you think the scientists cannot tell from a fossil?
   - ⓐ about how much the dinosaur weighed
   - ⓑ about how long the dinosaur was
   - ⓒ about how tall the dinosaur was
   - ⓓ whether the dinosaur hunted during the day or night

4. The opposite of *discovered* is . . .
   - ⓐ recovered.　　ⓑ uncovered.　　ⓒ unknown.　　ⓓ found.

5. What tells us that mammoths (furry elephants) lived at the same time as people?
   - ⓐ Some of the mammoths' fossil bones have arrow tips stuck in them.
   - ⓑ Cave people wrote about catching them.
   - ⓒ There are paintings of them in museums.
   - ⓓ Cave people sang about the mammoths.

6. Picture yourself looking at an actual dinosaur skeleton set up on display. Where are you?
   - ⓐ at a school　　　　ⓒ at a movie theater
   - ⓑ at a museum　　　　ⓓ at an amusement park

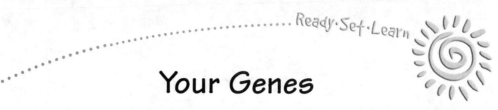

Your Genes

Do you have curly hair? Are you taller than other kids your age? These characteristics were decided before you were born. You got your traits from your parents. They passed their traits on to you through genes.

Genes carry codes for blue eyes or brown eyes. Genes say how tall you can get and what color hair you will have. You got half of your genes from your mother. You got half of your genes from your father. So you have your own set of genes. Each person gets different genes for each body part. That is why you look like—but not exactly like—your brother or sister.

Traits from a dominant gene show up most of the time. Brown eyes are dominant over blue eyes. Traits from a recessive gene show up less often. Light hair comes from a recessive gene. Dark hair is more common. Look at the eye color and hair color of the people around you. You will see that this is true.

Genes help to make you who you are. But they don't tell the whole story. Your genes may help you to be fast and strong. But you still need to learn how to run or swim or skate well.

Your Genes *(cont.)*

Directions: Fill in the bubble next to the best answer.

1. Traits from a recessive gene . . .
   ⓐ show up in most children.
   ⓑ do not show up in most children.
   ⓒ cannot show up in children.
   ⓓ will not be passed on by the parents.

2. What happened first?
   ⓐ You went to school.
   ⓑ You were born with brown eyes.
   ⓒ You got a set of genes from your parents.
   ⓓ You look like your grandmother.

3. One of Billy's grandparents has green eyes. All of the others have brown eyes. Both of Billy's parents have brown eyes. We can tell that Billy's eyes are probably . . .
   ⓐ recessive.　　ⓑ green.　　ⓒ dominant.　　ⓓ brown.

4. *Characteristics* means . . .
   ⓐ traits.　ⓑ dominant genes.　ⓒ recessive genes.　ⓓ codes.

5. Jan has a brother. They look a lot alike because . . .
   ⓐ they have none of the same genes.
   ⓑ they have many of the same genes.
   ⓒ they have the very same genes.
   ⓓ one is adopted.

6. Picture a forest of pine trees. A new pine tree growing at the forest's edge would probably look most like . . .
   ⓐ the pine trees in a forest miles away.
   ⓑ a fern.
   ⓒ a palm tree.
   ⓓ the pine trees nearby.

The Great Reef

The biggest coral reef in the world is near Australia. The Great Barrier Reef is the largest thing ever made by living beings. People call it one of the Seven Natural Wonders of the World.

The Great Barrier Reef lies just below the water's surface. It started forming about 500,000 years ago. Dead coral left behind their skeletons. New coral grew on top of the dead ones. This happened over and over again. Year after year the coral built up the reef. Today it is more than 1,250 miles (2,010 km) long. And it is still growing.

The coral come in many colors. Each coral forms a small part of the reef. Thousands of different animals live there. Fish and sea birds share the reef with giant clams, sea turtles, crabs, starfish, and many others.

A coral reef is alive. People must take care not to harm it. But many people broke off pieces of coral to sell or keep. They were hurting the reef. So in 1975 Australia made it against the law to take away any of the coral. They also made the reef a park.

Each year thousands of people come to see the reef. They want to swim around the reef. People can swim right up close to the coral. They can look at it. But they should not touch it. Now businesses think there may be oil in the area. They want to drill to find out. But Australia wants to keep the reef safe. So officers patrol the reef to make sure that the laws are followed.

26

The Great Reef (cont.)

Directions: Fill in the bubble next to the best answer.

1. What is the biggest thing ever made by living beings?
   ⓐ Australia
   ⓑ the Great Barrier Reef
   ⓒ the Seventh Wonder of the World
   ⓓ an ocean

2. What happened last?
   ⓐ Australia made the reef into a park.
   ⓑ People were breaking off pieces of coral.
   ⓒ Businesses wanted to drill for oil near the reef.
   ⓓ People were selling the coral.

3. Why is the reef still growing?
   ⓐ New layers of coral are always being added.
   ⓑ There are vitamins in the water.
   ⓒ When people break off pieces, it encourages the reef grow.
   ⓓ Australia has put in magnets that make the reef grow.

4. To patrol means . . .
   ⓐ to swim.   ⓑ to buy.   ⓒ to block off.   ⓓ to guard.

5. Why is Australia against drilling for oil near the reef?
   ⓐ The oil isn't needed.
   ⓑ It's not right for businesses to make money.
   ⓒ Some oil might get into the water and damage the reef.
   ⓓ People would lose interest in the reef.

6. Picture yourself swimming at the Great Barrier Reef. Which animal wouldn't you see?
   ⓐ seals   ⓑ sea turtles   ⓒ fish   ⓓ clams

Pony Express

When people moved west in covered wagons, things came slowly. Letters and news took a long time to get from one side of the country to the other. People had to wait for months to hear news from other places. Sometimes the mail took as long as one year, and other times it didn't arrive at all.

The Pony Express was established in 1860 to help mail and news move quickly from one place to another. Riders brought mail and messages to people who were willing to pay for it. The Pony Express gave the riders $100 dollars each month.

Each rider had to weigh less than 125 pounds. Larger people were not hired. Riders rode in rain or snow, day or night. They often rode in very dangerous conditions. Mail carriers had to ride very fast. They would change horses every 10–15 miles at a relay station. After 100 miles, a new rider would take over.

The Pony Express did not last long because it had many problems. The people who gave money to get it started did not get much money back. The letters cost too much to send. In 1862, the Pony Express ended.

Directions: Circle the letter next to the correct answer.

1. The Pony Express was . . .
   a. a place to keep ponies.
   b. horses and riders that carried mail and news across the U.S.
   c. a line of horses that had many names.
   d. a train named after a pony.

2. Which of the following could be dangers that a Pony Express rider probably faced?
   a. friendly pioneers
   b. calm streams and beautiful scenery
   c. wolves and Native American attacks
   d. wagon trains and campfires

3. If you wanted to ride for the Pony Express, how much could you weigh?
   a. less than 125 pounds   c. 155 pounds
   b. more than 125 pounds   d. weight didn't matter

Tropical Rainforests

Rainforests are very warm, wet forests. Rain falls for days and even months. Rainforests have millions of different types of plants and animals. They live in the four different zones of the rainforest.

The first zone is called the emergent zone. This is high above the rainforest. Here, giant trees stretch higher than the average height of any of the other plants. Many birds and insects live here.

The second zone is the canopy. This is the leafy area of the tops of the trees. Most of the animals in the rainforest live here. You can find monkeys, parrots, and frogs up here. You can also find butterflies, snakes, and sloths. A sloth is a very slow-moving animal that hangs upside down from the trees.

The understory is the third zone. It is made up of mostly young trees and shrubs. It is dark and cool. It is under the leaves, but not on the ground.

The forest floor is the final zone of the rainforest. The largest animals, such as jaguars and even elephants usually live here. The forest floor is also home to millions and millions of insects!

Directions: Circle the letter next to the correct answer.

1. In which zone would you most likely find a large animal such as a jaguar?
   a. emergent zone
   b. canopy
   c. understory
   d. forest floor

2. According to the passage, how many types of plants and animals live in the rainforest?
   a. trillions
   b. millions
   c. kazillions
   d. thousands

3. Which is the highest zone in the rainforest?
   a. forest floor
   b. emergent
   c. canopy
   d. understory

4. In this passage, *zone* probably means . . .
   a. time zone.
   b. area under water.
   c. part or section.
   d. area where no animals live.

Luna Moths

Most moths we see are very small. They are usually either white or brown. There are many other kinds of moths, but they are more rare. One beautiful type of moth is called the luna moth. "Luna" means moon. Like many moths, luna moths fly at night. In the moonlight they sometimes have a glowing green color.

The luna moth is actually a pale green. It has four spots, one on each wing. These spots sometimes look like eyes. The spots, or "eyes," are green, brown, and white. The luna moth is very large. It has long, sweeping lower tail wings. Once you have seen a luna moth, you will always recognize another luna moth by the spots, or eyes, or by the shape of its long tail wings.

The luna moth begins its life as a caterpillar. When it is a caterpillar, it is striped with green and yellow, and it has spines on its back. The caterpillar eats the leaves of hickory, walnut, sweet gum, and birch trees. Some types of luna moth caterpillars eat poison ivy! When it is time, the caterpillar makes a 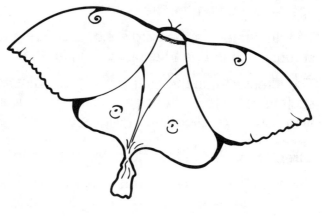 cocoon, where it lives until it turns into a moth.

You can tell a moth from a butterfly by looking closely at its antennae. A moth has soft, fuzzy antennae and a fuzzy body. A butterfly has antennae that look more like thin, dark wire. Moths are more visible at night. You usually see butterflies during the day.

In the United States, most luna moths live in the eastern part of the country. If you're lucky enough to live in this area, look into the moonlight at night and see if you can spot a luna moth flying around among the leafy green trees.

Luna Moths (cont.)

Directions: Read the story and circle the correct answer.

1. When do luna moths sometimes have a glowing green color?
   a. in the sunlight
   b. in the moonlight
   c. when they live in the eastern part of the country
   d. when they are very small

2. What are the spots on the luna moth's wings called?
   a. fuzzies
   b. antennae
   c. eyes
   d. wings

3. You can tell that it is unusual that . . .
   a. some types of luna moth caterpillars eat poison ivy.
   b. the luna moth flies at night.
   c. most moths are very small.
   d. the luna moth has soft, fuzzy antennae.

4. What is the main idea of this passage?
   a. "Luna" means moon.
   b. Luna moth caterpillars eat different types of leaves.
   c. Luna moths live mostly in the eastern part of the country.
   d. Luna moths are unique and beautiful.

5. A good way to answer the question number 4 would be to . . .
   a. think about the different moths you may have seen in your life.
   b. look in an encyclopedia under luna moths.
   c. notice what most of the passage is describing.
   d. read what the last paragraph has to say.

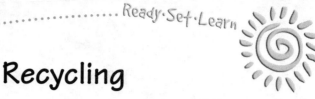

Recycling

Every day there is less and less space on Earth for trash. Yet every day we make more and more trash. What can we do? We can recycle some of our trash. Recycling means that the trash will be made into something that can be used again.

Recycling helps the Earth. And it saves space in trash dumps. Half of everything that we put into **landfills** could be recycled instead. In fact, most things made of paper, metal, aluminum, glass, and plastic can be recycled.

Paper can be ground up and made into new paper. Steel and aluminum cans can be melted down and made into new cans. The same is true of glass bottles. This can be done over and over again. Recycling doesn't take as much energy as making these things the first time. So, by recycling we can use less of the Earth's fuel resources.

Plastic can be melted down, too. Then it can be formed into park benches, fences, playgrounds, and lumber. Some people call plastic the "wood" of the future. Things made of plastic will last about 400 years—even if they stay outside in the weather. No wood can do that!

32

Recycling *(cont.)*

Directions: Fill in the bubble next to the best answer.

1. The main idea is . . .
   - ⓐ that we should recycle everything that we can.
   - ⓑ that we can build benches that last 400 years.
   - ⓒ that old newspapers can be reused.
   - ⓓ that cans should be melted.

2. What happens last?
   - ⓐ The can is put into a recycling bin.
   - ⓑ The can is melted down so it can be reused.
   - ⓒ A steel can gets filled with corn.
   - ⓓ A person uses the corn in the can.

3. What will happen if people begin to recycle all that they can?
   - ⓐ More of the Earth's resources will be used up.
   - ⓑ Things will cost less money.
   - ⓒ Trash dumps will fill up faster.
   - ⓓ Trash dumps won't fill up so fast.

4. What is a landfill?
   - ⓐ a factory
   - ⓑ a valley that's been filled in
   - ⓒ a place for garbage
   - ⓓ a recycling center

5. Plastic benches can last longer than wooden ones because . . .
   - ⓐ plastic cannot burn like wood.
   - ⓑ plastic cannot dissolve like wood.
   - ⓒ plastic cannot rust like wood.
   - ⓓ plastic cannot rot like wood.

6. Picture a dump. What do you see that cannot be recycled?
   - ⓐ a plastic milk jug
   - ⓑ an old couch
   - ⓒ a glass baby food jar
   - ⓓ a magazine with a torn cover

Ghost Town

An old town hides in the mountains of Montana. The name of it is Garnet. Most people today simply call it a ghost town. Many buildings still stand, but the town is silent. The last person who lived in the town of Garnet was a storeowner who died in 1947.

Garnet was started by families who came looking for gold in 1898. Over 1,000 people made their homes in the town. The men and women built the town by hand. Men worked hard inside the mines. They used simple hand tools and steam engines. Sixty thousand ounces of gold were mined near Garnet. Fifty thousand ounces of silver were found. Sixty thousand ounces of copper were put into mining cars.

The town was not built to last very long. After five years, the gold was almost gone. The copper was gone. Only a little silver remained. One hundred fifty people lived in the town at that point.

World War I took the men away from the town. People packed their bags. They took their families and moved away. A fire ruined most of the buildings in Garnet in 1912.

Garnet became a ghost town overnight. Today, the town of Garnet is full of history. It is a quiet place to walk around and hear whispers about life in the past.

Directions: Circle the letter next to the correct answer.

1. In this story, *mine* is a word for . . .
   a. something that belongs to me.
   b. ghost town.
   c. an underground area that is created to get minerals.
   d. silver and gold.

2. Garnet is now . . .
   a. a river town.   c. a mining town.
   b. a seaport town.   d. a ghost town.

3. Why did the city of Garnet die so suddenly?
   a. The gold ran out.   c. The men went to fight in World War I.
   b. The silver ran out.   d. all of the above

Forests

Forests can be found all around the world. There are many different plants and animals that use the forest as their home.

In the forest, small animals eat the fruits, nuts, mushrooms, and insects. They race around from tree to tree and jump from branch to branch. Larger animals eat smaller animals. Other animals eat seeds and shrubs. The forests are filled with animals. An ant, bat, robin, snake, deer, or turkey may be hiding among the leaves. They may be sitting in the trees. They might be running on the ground.

Many different types of trees live in the forest. Trees drop their leaves during the fall to save water on the floor of the forest. The soil is made up of fallen leaves, dirt, and animals that have died. After the animals and plants die, their bodies break down. This makes the earth rich with nutrients.

Forests are fun places to visit. A person who wants to see and hear the real sounds of the forest must sit quietly and listen with his or her eyes and ears.

Directions: Circle the letter next to the correct answer.

1. Which type of area is the article describing?
   a. mountains   b. ocean   c. desert   d. forest

2. If you were to close your eyes in the forest, which one of these sounds might you hear?
   a. a squirrel chattering with its friend   c. waves crashing on the rocks
   b. breaking glass   d. seagulls screeching

3. The purpose of this passage is . . .
   a. to entertain the reader with forest crafts he or she can make.
   b. to inform the reader of interesting facts about a forest.
   c. to persuade the reader to travel to a forest on vacation.
   d. to encourage the reader to create his or her own forest.

4. A good **synonym** for the word *shrub* could be . . .
   a. dog.   c. bird.
   b. bush.   d. sand.

The Dust Bowl

During the 1930s, the people who lived in the Midwest had a big problem: Oklahoma and parts of Kansas, Texas, Colorado, and New Mexico had terrible dust storms. A reporter called the area the Dust Bowl. The name stuck. With so much dust in the air, sheep and cattle choked to death. People got very sick. Some even died. If enough dust collected in a home's attic, the ceiling fell in. Many farms were completely ruined. So farmers packed up their families and left. They headed to California, hoping to find work. More than 500,000 people left the Dust Bowl.

What caused the Dust Bowl? It wasn't just one thing. During the 1920s, farmers got tractors for the first time. That meant that they could plow much more land than ever before. They got rid of all the trees. And they plowed miles and miles of straight rows to plant their crops. Then there was a lack of rain. Everything got very dry. The crops died. To make things worse, winds up to 70 miles per hour picked up lots of the dry dirt. Since there were no trees to slow down the wind, tons of dirt blew away. Sometimes the dirt landed as far away as Washington, D.C.!

After years of bad dust storms and no rain, the government decided to help the farmers. The Department of Agriculture told farmers to plant crops in rows that ran against the wind. The government gave the farmers money to plant trees between fields. It also helped them to find ways to water their crops when the rains didn't come.

The Dust Bowl *(cont.)*

Directions: Fill in the bubble next to the best answer.

1. Which state was not a part of the Dust Bowl?
   - ⓐ California
   - ⓑ Oklahoma
   - ⓒ Kansas
   - ⓓ New Mexico

2. What happened first?
   - ⓐ The crops died.
   - ⓑ The Department of Agriculture helped farmers.
   - ⓒ Farmers got rid of all of the trees.
   - ⓓ There were dust storms.

3. What happened because the farmers plowed straight rows in line with the wind?
   - ⓐ No rain fell.
   - ⓑ Crops died.
   - ⓒ It got too hot.
   - ⓓ The wind picked up the soil and blew it away.

4. Another word for *agriculture* is . . .
   - ⓐ health.
   - ⓑ farming.
   - ⓒ money.
   - ⓓ water.

5. How did tractors help bring about the Dust Bowl?
   - ⓐ Tractors kept water from reaching the crops.
   - ⓑ Tractors let farmers plow much more land than they could before.
   - ⓒ Tractors made crops die.
   - ⓓ The tractor wheels picked up the dust and threw it in the air.

6. Picture yourself standing in the Dust Bowl after a dust storm. No matter where you look, what color do you see?
   - ⓐ white   ⓑ green   ⓒ red   ⓓ brown

Penguins

Emperor penguins are birds. But they cannot fly. Instead, they swim. They use their "wings" as flippers to move through the water. They swim in the icy seas around Antarctica. When they are in the water, they stay in big groups. They call to each other to find the fish, krill, and squid they eat. Being in a group helps keep them safer from the leopard seals that want to eat them.

Adult emperor penguins are about the same size as you. They are about 4 feet (1.2 m) tall and weigh about 70 pounds (30 kg). When penguins are on shore, they cluster together in big groups called rookeries. Rookeries may have thousands of penguins. There the penguins pick their mates.

In the winter when it is dark and very, very cold, each mother penguin lays one egg on the ice. The father quickly pulls the egg into an opening near his feet called a broodpouch. Then the mother goes to find food. She stays out at sea for two months. During that time all of the fathers stay close together to keep from getting too cold. They also have a layer of fat to keep them warm. They must stand over their eggs for two months without ever leaving them. They eat no food. They must live off their body fat.

After the egg hatches, the chick stays in the father's broodpouch. This keeps it warm. At last the mother returns with food for the chick. She spits up food she has eaten. She spits the food into the baby penguin's hungry mouth. Then the mother tucks her chick into her own broodpouch. After four months, the chick can swim and get its own food.

Penguins (cont.)

Directions: Fill in the bubble next to the best answer.

1. What animal wants to eat the Emperor penguin?
   - ⓐ fish
   - ⓑ leopard seal
   - ⓒ krill
   - ⓓ squid

2. What happens last?
   - ⓐ The baby penguin hatches.
   - ⓑ The father penguin keeps the egg warm.
   - ⓒ The mother penguin goes out to sea.
   - ⓓ The mother penguin lays an egg.

3. How are penguins like most birds?
   - ⓐ They live in Antarctica.
   - ⓑ They build nests.
   - ⓒ They lay eggs.
   - ⓓ They fly.

4. A word that means the opposite of *cluster* is . . .
   - ⓐ scatter.　　ⓑ gather.　　ⓒ run.　　ⓓ sleep.

5. What does the male penguin probably do when his mate brings food for the baby?
   - ⓐ keeps the baby in his broodpouch
   - ⓑ attacks his mate
   - ⓒ steals the baby's food
   - ⓓ goes to sea to get his own food

6. Picture Antarctica on a globe. Emperor penguins live . . .
   - ⓐ north of the Equator.
   - ⓑ south of the Equator.
   - ⓒ near the Equator.
   - ⓓ at the North Pole.

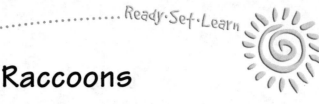

Raccoons

Raccoons are cute and clever. People love their little masked faces and their comical antics. Raccoons can solve problems, and they can make messes. A raccoon can open the lid on a trashcan. Some have even opened entire garage doors!

Raccoons live in forests. They climb trees and live in nests in tree trunks. They can fish and hunt for food. Raccoons also live in cities and near homes. They live in parks and backyards. They travel through waterways and eat trash.

People should carefully wrap trash that contains food. Raccoons feast on scraps of bread, vegetables, meats, and sweets. Put these "treats" in tied plastic bags and put the bags in a strong trashcan. Make sure the lid is tight, or a raccoon might snack at your house this evening!

Raccoons are messy. They scatter food scraps, paper, cans, and other trash in yards and other areas. Would you like to clean up after a raccoon?

Raccoons look sweet—but beware. People think they are cuddly, but raccoons are wild animals. Raccoons are dangerous. They have sharp teeth and claws. They can carry diseases. Never approach a wild raccoon. They are cute, but they are not pets.

Directions: Circle the letter next to the correct answer.

1. Where do raccoons live?
   a. only in forests
   b. only near people
   c. neither in forests nor near people
   d. in forests and near people

2. What are some of the negative things raccoons do?
   a. They damage property and shred paper.
   b. They can open your lids and doors.
   c. They tear trash out of cans.
   d. all of the above

3. If you gave the passage a new title, it could be . . .
   a. "Battle Over Raccoons.
   b. "Keeping Your Own Raccoon."
   c. "How to Care for a Raccoon of Your Own."
   d. "Raccoons Are Clever but Dangerous."

Oceans

The ocean is an amazing part of our Earth. There are many parts to it and many different types of animals that live in it.

Coral reefs give food and shelter to small animals that live near the top of the water. Coral reefs are warm and usually have plenty of light. Starfish, sea anemones, and clams live here.

The seashore is the part of the ocean most of us know best. It includes the sand and the tide pools along the rocks. Animals that live on the rocks have special arms and legs that help them hold onto the rocks when the waves crash over them. Other animals, like crabs and some birds, move every time the waves crash back and forth. Smaller animals stay alive by quickly digging holes into the sand.

Many animals and plants live in the open ocean where the waters still have some light. Sharks, fish, turtles, and seals live there.

In the deepest parts of the ocean, it is very cold and completely dark. Some animals that live down there actually create their own light to attract other fish!

Directions: Circle the letter next to the correct answer.

1. Why would you probably not find a coral reef in the deep ocean?
   a. Reefs need cold water to live.
   b. Reefs need light and warm water to live.
   c. Reefs need to live in dark parts of the ocean.
   d. Reefs wouldn't have enough food in the deep.

2. How do some of the smaller sand animals survive on the seashore?
   a. They grab onto the coral reef.
   b. They roll with the waves.
   c. They hold on to rocks.
   d. They tunnel quickly down into the sand.

3. According to the passage, what can some animals that live in the deep ocean do?
   a. They can go for long periods of time without eating.
   b. They can create their own light.
   c. They can swim with their eyes closed.
   d. They can eat animals larger than themselves.

The Water Below

When snow melts, where does all the water go? How about when it rains? Much of the water runs off into streams and rivers. Some of it drains down through the dirt. Then it settles in a layer of gravel or sand. This area where the water settles is called an aquifer. People drill down to the aquifer. Then they pump the water up. They need the water for drinking and cooking. They water their lawns. They wash their clothes and cars. They take baths and do dishes. About 1/5 of the fresh water used in America comes from aquifers. Many places that are far from lakes or rivers use only ground water.

The amount of ground water is called the water table. When more water is taken out than is replaced by rain or melting snow, the water table drops. This has happened in Arizona. In many other places, people are using up the ground water much too fast. The water tables are getting very low. This causes big problems. Sometimes the land cracks and sinks. Then roads and buildings are damaged. In New Jersey and other places along the coasts, salt water from the ocean has refilled the water table. But no one can use the salt water. The salt must be taken out first.

Aquifers near cities can have problems with pollution. The water may get filled with bad things. These things flow into the ground from trash dumps and sewer leaks. Dirty road run-off, chemicals, and farm fertilizers can get into an aquifer and cause problems, too.

42

The Water Below *(cont.)*

Directions: Fill in the bubble next to the best answer.

1. Why do people drill for aquifers?
   - ⓐ They want to find a good place to fish.
   - ⓑ They want to find a special kind of rock.
   - ⓒ They want to find fresh water.
   - ⓓ They want to find salt water.

2. What happens last?
   - ⓐ The sea water refills the water table.
   - ⓑ Salt must be removed from the water so it can be used.
   - ⓒ People use too much ground water.
   - ⓓ People discover an aquifer.

3. Chemicals in an aquifer are a form of . . .
   - ⓐ water pollution.
   - ⓑ water table.
   - ⓒ water ecology.
   - ⓓ water conservation.

4. The word *damaged* means the same as . . .
   - ⓐ sad.   ⓑ lost.   ⓒ changed.   ⓓ harmed.

5. Which would not cause problems for an aquifer?
   - ⓐ a lack of rain
   - ⓑ people wasting water
   - ⓒ people going to the beach
   - ⓓ a landfill leak

6. Picture a pump bringing water up from underground. What else do people pump up from underground?
   - ⓐ lava   ⓑ oil   ⓒ mud   ⓓ tree roots

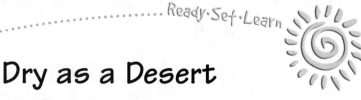

Dry as a Desert

You may think that a desert is always a hot place. But did you know that Antarctica is a desert? A desert can be stony or sandy or even icy. It can have mountains or be flat. But in all deserts, almost all of the water is under the ground. And it hardly ever rains. All deserts are very dry.

Africa has the world's biggest desert. The Sahara Desert is so big that it crosses 12 countries. During the day it has gotten as hot as 136°F (58°C)! The ground can reach 165°F (74°C). Then at night it gets freezing cold! Most of the deserts of the world follow this pattern.

The hot desert is a **harsh** environment. The plants that live there grow slowly. They have very long roots to seek out water. Few animals live in a desert. Those that do, spend their days in holes deep under the ground. After sunset, they come out to look for food. Many of the animals that hunt other animals are poisonous. That's because they don't often run into something to eat. So when they do, they must kill it.

The cold desert of Antarctica is also a tough place to live. It is covered by ice and snow all year long. There are high winds. Still, tiny plants such as bacteria, algae, and moss live there. So do insects, penguins, seals, birds, and fish.

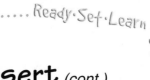

Dry as a Desert *(cont.)*

Directions: Fill in the bubble next to the best answer.

1. What do all deserts have in common?
   ⓐ They are very hot.
   ⓑ They are sandy.
   ⓒ They are flat.
   ⓓ They are very dry.

2. What happens during 24 hours in a typical desert?
   ⓐ It is hot all day and all night.
   ⓑ It is hot all day and then cold at night.
   ⓒ It is cold all day and then hot at night.
   ⓓ It is cold all day and all night.

3. Compared to the Sahara Desert, all other deserts are . . .
   ⓐ smaller.
   ⓑ bigger.
   ⓒ hotter.
   ⓓ colder.

4. The opposite of *harsh* is . . .
   ⓐ warm.   ⓒ pleasant.
   ⓑ cold.   ⓓ difficult.

5. How does poison help desert animals?
   ⓐ The poison keeps them cooler.
   ⓑ The poison keeps them from needing water.
   ⓒ The poison helps them to see better at night.
   ⓓ The poison makes their bite more deadly.

6. Picture a hot desert just after the sun sets. What don't you see?
   ⓐ a stream
   ⓑ plants
   ⓒ animals
   ⓓ sand

Sea Turtles

Turtles have lived on Earth for more than 185 million years. They have changed little in all that time. All turtles can see, feel, and smell. Sea turtles are some of the biggest ones. They live in warm oceans worldwide.

Hard scales cover sea turtles' heads. They have no teeth. But they have powerful jaws to grab and tear food. Sea turtles do not have feet. They have flippers.

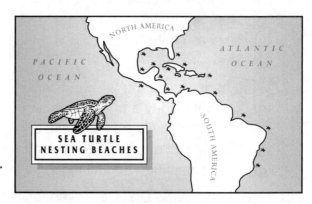

SEA TURTLE
NESTING BEACHES

Bony plates form a turtle's shell. It is part of the skeleton. Sea turtles cannot pull their heads and legs into their shells. They are too big. They must rely on speed to get away from danger. They move their flippers like a bird flaps its wings. Sea turtles swim faster than all other turtles. Some can go 20 miles per hour for a short time! But on land, sea turtles move slowly. Males never leave the water. Females only do so to lay eggs.

A female may swim thousands of miles to reach a breeding beach. When she does, she digs a hole in the beach. She uses her back feet. She lays up to 200 eggs in the hole. She covers them with sand. Then she returns to the water.

The sun warms the eggs. They hatch. The tiny turtles must drag themselves across the beach to the water. It is the most dangerous time of their lives. Many animals eat newborn turtles. Only one of every three baby turtles reaches the sea.

Now shrimp nets are a big threat to sea turtles. Each year around the world 155,000 sea turtles drown in these nets.

Ready·Set·Learn

Sea Turtles *(cont.)*

Directions: Circle the letter next to each correct answer.

1. Where do sea turtles live?
   a. in fresh-water lakes
   b. in cold sea water
   c. in warm sea water

2. For a short while a sea turtle can swim at a speed of . . .
   a. 2 miles per hour.
   b. 20 miles per hour.
   c. 200 miles per hour.

3. How are shrimp nets bad for sea turtles?
   a. Sea turtles get caught in the nets and drown.
   b. The nets block the nesting beaches so sea turtles can't reach them.
   c. The nets are used to gather up baby sea turtles for food.

4. A sea turtle cannot pull its head or legs into its shell. True or false? Tell why.

   _____

   _____

   _____

   _____

   _____

   _____

   _____

   _____

Rainbow Soup

You can eat a rainbow if you put it in soup! Before you start, be sure to check and see if you have everything you need. And, most importantly, ask a grown-up to help with the stove!

Rainbow Soup

This recipe makes enough for two hungry people. You will need the following:

Rainbow Vegetables
- ½ cup celery, chopped into little bits
- 1 small carrot, cut into thin slices
- 1 medium-sized tomato, chopped
- 2 green onion tops, cut into small pieces

Noodles and Chicken
- 1 cup cooked multi-colored bow-tie noodles
- ½ cup cooked chicken, cut into tiny, bite-size pieces
- 3 cups chicken broth

Directions
1. Put the broth into a one-quart soup pot.
2. Add the rainbow vegetables to the broth. Do not add the onion tops yet.
3. Bring the broth to a boil.
4. Cover the pot with a lid and turn the heat to low.
5. Cook for 20 minutes.
6. Take the lid off of the pot. Add the rainbow noodles, chicken, and onion tops into the pot.
7. Simmer for 2–3 minutes or until the chicken and noodles are hot.

When the soup is ready, put it in a bowl. Now you and a friend can enjoy rainbow soup together.

Rainbow Soup *(cont.)*

Directions: Read the story and circle the correct answer.

1. What is the first step in the instructions?
   a. Cook the chicken.
   b. Put the broth into a pot.
   c. Put the noodles into a pot.
   d. Put the soup in two bowls.

2. After you cover the pot with a lid and turn the heat to low, how long should the broth cook?
   a. 2–3 minutes.
   b. 10 minutes.
   c. 20 minutes.
   d. 1 hour.

3. When will you need to add the noodles, chicken, and onion tops?
   a. After the broth begins to boil.
   b. After you put the broth into a one-quart soup pot.
   c. After the broth has cooked for 20 minutes.
   d. After the broth has simmered for 2–3 minutes.

4. A good way to answer the question right above this one is to . . .
   a. think about how long it takes water to boil.
   b. quickly skim over the recipe and directions.
   c. pay close attention to each step of the directions.
   d. look at a picture of the soup in a cookbook.

5. The directions in this passage are about how to . . .
   a. spot rainbows.
   b. enjoy soup with a friend.
   c. cook chicken.
   d. make rainbow soup.

AYSO Soccer

Have you ever wanted to kick a soccer ball? Have you ever wanted to play on a soccer team? AYSO soccer may be just the place for you. It is one of the largest soccer programs in the U.S.

What does AYSO mean? AYSO stands for "American Youth Soccer Organization." It is a club that is in all 50 states. AYSO has five simple things it believes in.

The most important idea is that everyone plays. All players must play at least half of every game. This makes them feel like they are an important part of the team.

The second belief is to have balanced teams. Teams that play each other should be made up of players that have the same amount of experience.

The third belief of AYSO is to have open registration. This means everyone is allowed to play. As long as a child is between the ages of 4–19, he or she can play.

Positive coaching is the fourth belief. Coaches in AYSO make soccer fun, as well as a learning time. Children learn how play like a team.

The last belief is that all players should be good sports. They should respect each other. Children learn that winning is not the most important thing. Being a good sport and doing your best is what playing in AYSO is all about.

Directions: Circle the letter next to the correct answer.

1. The word *organization* means the same as . . .
   a. game.   b. soccer ball.   c. house.   d. group or club.

2. Who can play in AYSO?
   a. children ages one to three   c. adults ages 40–50
   b. children ages 4–19   d. only girls

3. The author's purpose for this passage is . . .
   a. to entertain the reader with soccer jokes.
   b. to inform the reader about the rules of the soccer player.
   c. to persuade the reader to kick a soccer ball on weekends.
   d. to inform the reader about the five beliefs of the AYSO.

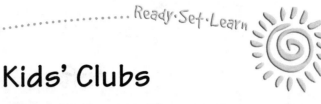

Kids' Clubs

Clubs are great ways to meet people your age. They are also a way to enjoy many different exciting activities.

Girl Scouts of America is a program for girls. They can be 5–17 years in age. Girls meet every week of the school year. They learn to help out in the community. They learn to work as a team. They build life skills. They make friends. They build strong values and find out what makes them special.

Boy Scouts of America is for boys. Boy Scouts teach character. They teach the boys to be responsible citizens. They learn survival skills. Also, boys learn to build strong bodies. Boy Scouts are from 5–17 years old.

Awana Club is a club for both boys and girls. It is like Boy Scouts and Girl Scouts. Boys and girls from 3–17 may go to Awana. It meets every week of the school year. They learn to be responsible citizens. They do community service. They learn to build strong morals. They learn to develop character. There are contests and games each year.

Girls Scouts, Boy Scouts, and Awana Club are just three of the many types of clubs available to you. Join one today!

Directions: Circle the letter next to the correct answer.

1. What are all three clubs interested in building?
   a. strong buildings   c. strong values
   b. strong bodies   d. strong clubs

2. A synonym for the word *join* could be . . .
   a. quit.   b. make.   c. enter.   d. draw.

3. The author's purpose for this passage is to . . .
   a. entertain the reader with funny, new information.
   b. inform the reader about clubs that he or she might be interested in joining.
   c. persuade the reader to attend Boy Scouts.
   d. none of the above.

4. Boy and Girl Scouts have kids from the ages of . . .
   a. 0–9.   b. 5–17.   c. 6–19.   d. 5–30.

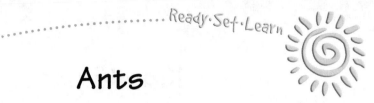

Ants

Ants are incredible creatures. Each colony has its own smell. Each of the ants in the colony knows the smell. Enemies will not be able to enter their camp without being discovered. Several types of ants have a sting to protect their nests when intruders turn up.

The queen ant is the only one who can lay eggs for the colony. None of the other ants can lay eggs at all.

The worker ants cannot lay eggs. They take care of newborn ants. They also search for food. These worker ants protect their nest from enemies. They also keep the nest tidy. They take out the "trash" from the nest and place it in one area.

Slave-maker ants rob the nest of other ants. They steal the pupae, the cases that hold the ant eggs. Then they bring the pupae back to their camp. When the stolen cases hatch, these stolen ants become slaves.

Finally, all ants have antennas and jaws. They need antennas for smelling and touching. They have strong, long jaws. They open and shut sideways like pairs of scissors. Adult ants cannot chew and swallow food, so they squeeze the food until the juice comes out. They swallow the juice and throw away the leftover dried parts of the food.

Ant colonies must have worker ants and slave-maker ants. They must also have a queen ant to lay eggs. They must have a way to catch other ants that try to get into their nest. Without a queen to lay eggs, or antennae to hear and touch and jaws to tear food, there would be no ant colonies left in the world.

Directions: Circle the letter next to the correct answer.

1. According to the text, what are pupae?
   a. the cases that hold the ant eggs   c. adult ants
   b. baby ants   d. worker ants

2. Using the context above, another term for *intruders* would be . . .
   a. unwanted friends.   c. unwanted enemies.
   b. unwanted vacationers.   d. unwanted slaves.

Hummingbirds

Hummingbirds are amazing birds for many reasons. They fly like helicopters: backwards or floating in the air. They move from side to side. The hummingbirds zoom straight up into the sky or dive straight down. They spin their wings in circles. If their babies are in danger, they will even attack eagles. To build nests, they will pick fuzz off your sweater.

When they are awake, hummingbirds spend most of their day eating. They are always on a quest for insects to eat. They need them for protein. Hummingbirds are also always looking for objects from which to drink juice. They fly into brightly-colored objects that they think are food. Every day they visit up to 1,000 flowers to drink the juice! Sometimes they even try to get juice from stop signs!

Hummingbirds have special tongues. The fronts of their tongues are split in half and have sharp edges. These edges help soak up juice from flowers. Their tongues lick flowers. As they hunt for insects, this tongue grabs the bugs and insects quickly.

Its unique tongue, flying, and eating habits are just three of the things that make the hummingbird an unbelievable creature.

Directions: Circle the letter next to the correct letter.

1. According to the passage, what is one way in which hummingbirds are amazing?
   a. They make a great deal of noise.   c. They can fly like a helicopter.
   b. They are very small and delicate.   d. They can drink water.

2. In the text, "a quest for insects" means . . .
   a. questions about.   b. ability.   c. journey.   d. search.

3. The author's purpose for this passage is to . . .
   a. entertain the reader with interesting hummingbird characteristics.
   b. inform the reader about dangerous hummingbirds.
   c. persuade the reader to purchase a hummingbird.
   d. encourage the reader to keep insects in their garden.

Hot Cocoa

Arturo and Carlos have been playing outside. They're cold, cold, cold! Their mother tells them to take a hot bath. Then she shows them how to make hot cocoa! Yum!

Hot Cocoa

Food You Will Need:
- ⅓ cup sugar
- ⅓ cup unsweetened cocoa powder
- dash salt
- ⅓ cup water
- 3½ cups milk
- ½ teaspoon vanilla

Equipment You Will Need:
- 1½-quart pan
- measuring cups and spoons
- wooden spoon
- whisk
- 4 cups

Directions

1. In the pan, mix sugar, cocoa, and salt. Slowly stir in the water. Put pan on the stove. With help from an adult, turn the burner to medium heat. Cook and stir until the mixture boils. Boil one minute, stirring all the time.

2. Add the milk, one cup at a time, stirring as you do. Heat and stir until the mixture starts to bubble around the edge of the pan. Turn off the burner. With help from an adult, move the pan off the stove. Stir in the vanilla.

3. Use the whisk to beat the mixture until foamy. Be careful not to splatter it. Pour it into the cups.

54

Hot Cocoa (cont.)

Directions: Read the story and circle the correct answer.

1. When should you add the milk?
   a. after you stir in the vanilla
   b. after the mixture has boiled for one minute
   c. after you pour the hot cocoa into the cups
   d. before you add anything else

2. When should you turn off the burner?
   a. after you use the whisk to beat the mixture
   b. whenever you feel like it
   c. after you drink the hot cocoa
   d. when the mixture starts to bubble around the edge of the pan

3. What is another good name for this treat?
   a. "Yummy Winter Drink"
   b. "Milk and Vanilla"
   c. "Boiled Water"
   d. "Drinking Cocoa Powder"

4. A good reason to have an adult help you when you make this treat is that . . .
   a. hot burners and hot drinks can burn you.
   b. it is more fun to work with someone else.
   c. it takes two people to do all the work.
   d. a child needs help when measuring sugar.

5. The writer probably wrote this recipe to . . .
   a. tell you what Arturo and Carlos usually do.
   b. warn you to turn off burners.
   c. warn you about cold winters.
   d. tell you how to make hot cocoa.

Hospital Technology

Many scientists today are trying to discover new ways to help doctors, nurses, and patients in hospitals. They are trying to create new machines that help to ease the pain of patients and make doctors' and nurses' jobs easier.

One machine that is helping patients is called a video remote interpreter, or VRI. It is a machine that helps people who are deaf. This machine connects to people outside the hospital who can help the deaf person communicate with the doctors and nurses.

Another machine is being made for people with bad burns. This machine will be set up next to the hospital bed. It will be close to, but not touching, the patient. This is important, as people with burns are often in a lot of pain. It hurts them even more to have the burns touched. Usually a doctor or nurse needs to take a sample of the burn. They need to get a part of the skin from the burn. They do this so they can test for infection. Getting the sample is painful for the patient. This machine will be able to test a burn for infection by using the air around the burn. It will not touch the skin of the patient.

Scientists are working every day to invent new technology for hospitals. They want to help people who are sick. They want to help people stay healthy.

Directions: Circle the letter next to the correct answer.

1. VRI stands for…
   a. Very Runny Ink.
   b. Very Realistic Intelligence.
   c. Virtual Running Image.
   d. Video Remote Interpreter.

2. Which word could be a synonym for *sample*?
   a. skin
   b. piece
   c. arm
   d. leg

3. Why did the scientists try to make a machine that can work near the burn patient?
   a. so it can hum for the sick person
   b. so it can make a new noise
   c. so it can read the air and check for infections
   d. so it can watch the patient

4. A VRI is used for patients who are . . .
   a. blind.
   b. burned
   c. in a lot of pain.
   d. deaf.

Ready·Set·Learn

Saving the Movies

The first movies were made using black-and-white cameras. The film for the pictures were cut up and made into long strips. They were played on a movie projector in a theater. Today, people can see movies almost anywhere. They can see movies on computers. Others watch movies on iPods®. Some even watch movies on their cell phones. The world of movies is changing very fast.

Some filmmakers want to use digital photography for making movies. Digital photography is cheaper. It is easy to use and can be done in a small area. However, they do not turn out as clear as the original way of filming.

A man named Robert Rodriguez says that digital form is the new way to make movies. He says it is the way to keep movie theaters alive. He does not want them to become extinct.

Robert writes movies and shoots them. He directs them and puts them together. He even does the special effects. Robert does them all in digital format. He does this in his own home in Texas. He can make most movies for half of the money it would usually cost.

Rodriguez wants to make movies that can be seen only in theaters. His idea is to make movies, for less money, only to be shown in theaters. He feels this will help preserve the original way to watch a movie.

Directions: Circle the letter next to the correct answer.

1. What makes Robert unusual?
   a. He is trying to save the movie theaters.
   b. He is making movies.
   c. He only wants to make movies that can be shown on television.
   d. He is the only filmmaker who lives in Texas.

2. Which of these is NOT something positive about digital movies?
   a. They need fewer people to make them.
   b. They cost less than making movies the old way.
   c. They can be made using only a small amount of space.
   d. They are not as clear as the other kind.

Horses Helped Humans

Long ago horses were wild animals. They lived in Europe and Asia. Then people got the idea to tame them. Horses are smart. They can be trained. They are strong, too. Horses are strong enough for a person to ride. Horses can pull heavy loads. They can move much faster than a person can. So hunters on horses could catch more animals. They brought home more food. Horses also helped to win wars. Soldiers fought on horseback. The people without horses would often lose.

There were no horses in America 600 years ago. Then explorers came. They brought horses with them on ships. Some of these horses ran away. They formed herds of wild horses. The Native Americans saw these new animals. They saw that they were fast and strong. They decided to catch them and train them. After that the Native Americans rode horses, too.

For thousands of years horses were the best way to move on land. They were the fastest, too. Today, horses are not often used for transportation. In most places cars, buses, and trains are the best ways to travel on land.

Now people ride horses mostly for sport and fun. Some horses do work. Ranchers ride horses to round up cattle. Police horses carry officers through the streets of some cities. Horses pull people in carriages, sleighs, and hay wagons, too.

Horses Helped Humans *(cont.)*

Directions: Fill in the bubble next to the best answer.

1. The main idea is about . . .
   - ⓐ new forms of transportation.
   - ⓑ explorers needing horses.
   - ⓒ how horses are useful to people.
   - ⓓ how Native Americans got horses.

2. What happened first?
   - ⓐ Horses came over in ships.
   - ⓑ People in Europe and Asia tamed horses.
   - ⓒ Some horses ran away.
   - ⓓ The Native Americans had horses.

3. Horses are no longer ridden for . . .
   - ⓐ fun.
   - ⓑ sport.
   - ⓒ cattle ranches.
   - ⓓ battles.

4. *Transportation* means . . .
   - ⓐ moving people and things from one place to another.
   - ⓑ selling things in a store.
   - ⓒ going on a vacation.
   - ⓓ things that fly.

5. Why aren't horses used very much for transportation anymore?
   - ⓐ People don't like horses.
   - ⓑ People can get places faster with motors.
   - ⓒ Horses cost too much to feed.
   - ⓓ Horses have returned to the wild.

6. Picture the ships that brought horses to America. What kind were they?
   - ⓐ speed boats
   - ⓒ wooden with sails
   - ⓑ steamships
   - ⓓ rowboats

A Haunted House?

The rain was pounding on the roof as I tried to sleep. It sounded like a downpour. We had just moved into our new house. It wasn't really new, but it seemed new to us. Our old house was too small since Mom had the baby, so we had bought a new house right up the street.

The problem was that all the neighbors said the new house was haunted. All my friends teased me when they found out we were moving. I just let their words go in one ear and out the other.

Suddenly, I sat straight up in bed. Something was moving outside my window. Lying back down, my mind started to imagine things. Shadows moved across my wall, lightning flashed outside the window. Suddenly, a light shone on my window and my nightlight flickered and went out.

Several minutes later, a moaning sound came from outside my door. I jumped out of bed, put my feet into my warm, fuzzy slippers, and grabbed my baseball bat. Whatever it was, it was not going to frighten me again.

I reached for the door handle and started to open it.

"Boo!" yelled my big brother Alfred. He was standing in the hall with a long stick with a lantern on the end. He was wearing dark glasses and a long, black rain jacket.

"Did I scare you?" he asked.

Directions: Circle the letter next to the correct answer

1. "In one ear and out the other" is an idiom meaning . . .
   a. not really paying attention to what's being said.
   b. using a cotton swab to clean your ears.
   c. putting things in one ear and pull it out the other.
   d. putting something in and pulling it out.

2. Why did the kids at school tease the person telling the story?
   a. They knew the house's previous owner, and he was creepy.
   b. They were scared of the big windows in the new house.
   c. They were jealous that their parents hadn't bought the house.
   d. They said the new house was haunted.

Jelly Bean Planet

The rain was coming down heavily as I stood on the balcony of our apartment. It rained every day on our planet. Whenever I walked in the rain, I just opened my mouth to taste blueberry, raspberry, or a touch of licorice. The rain was delicious.

Running back inside to get out of the rain, I flopped onto the couch. It smelled of strawberries and cream. The pillow smelled like orange marmalade. Everywhere I walked, everything I did, fruity smells reached my nose.

I looked at the buildings outside our windows. There were tall blue ones, short green ones, and yellow oval ones as far as the eye could see. Some of the buildings had crazy patterns of several colors swirled on the sides. Fruity colors were everywhere.

"Breakfast, Son," my dad called. "It's jelly beans on toast and pancakes with jelly bean syrup."

"Awesome!" I bellowed from upstairs. "I'll be right there!"

Bounding down the stairs, I heard Mom calling, "Would you like a peanut butter sandwich with blackberry jelly beans or one with cherry?"

"Cherry," I called. "By the way, Mom, could you throw in the chocolate jelly bean cake for lunch?"

"This is delicious!" exclaimed Dad. "The only thing wrong with this planet is the dentist bill every month!"

Directions: Circle the letter next to the correct answer.

1. Why was everything sweet on this planet?
    a. It was the land of pie.
    b. It was only sweet on the weekdays.
    c. Part of it was made of jelly beans.
    d. There was too much chocolate.

2. A synonym for *bellowed* could be . . .
    a. shouted.   c. said.
    b. whispered.   d. guessed.

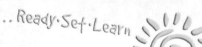

Answer Key

Page 5
1. a   3. a   5. c
2. a   4. a

Page 6
1. c   2. d   3. a   4. b

Page 7
1. c   2. c   3. b   4. c

Page 9
1. d   3. b   5. b
2. a   4. a

Page 11
1. b   3. a   5. a
2. a   4. d

Page 13
1. b   3. a   5. a
2. d   4. b

Page 15
1. b
2. a
3. c
4. Africa and India; Africa
5. Answers will vary.

Page 17
1. a   3. b   5. d
2. c   4. b   6. d

Page 19
1. a   3. c   5. d
2. c   4. d   6. b

Page 20
1. d   2. a   3. c   4. b

Page 21
1. b   2. c   3. c

Page 23
1. c   3. d   5. b
2. a   4. c   6. b

Page 25
1. b   3. d   5. b
2. c   4. a   6. d

Page 27
1. b   3. a   5. c
2. a   4. d   6. a

Page 28
1. b   2. c   3. a

Page 29
1. d   2. b   3. b   4. c

Page 31
1. b   3. a   5. c
2. c   4. d

Page 33
1. a   3. d   5. b
2. b   4. c   6. b

Page 34
1. c   2. d   3. d

Page 35
1. d   2. a   3. b   4. b

Page 37
1. a   3. d   5. b
2. c   4. b   6. d

Page 39
1. b   3. c   5. d
2. a   4. a   6. b

Page 40
1. d   2. d   3. d

Page 41
1. b   2. d   3. b

Page 43
1. c   3. a   5. c
2. b   4. d   6. b

Page 45
1. d   3. a   5. d
2. b   4. c   6. a

Page 47
1. c
2. b
3. a
4. True. They are too big.

Page 49
1. b   3. c   5. d
2. c   4. c

Page 50
1. d   2. b   3. d

Page 51
1. c   2. c   3. b   4. b

Page 52
1. a   2. c

Page 53
1. c   2. d   3. a

Page 55
1. b   3. a   5. d
2. d   4. a

Page 56
1. d   2. b   3. c   4. d

Page 57
1. a   2. d

Page 59
1. c   3. d   5. b
2. b   4. a   6. c

Page 60
1. a   2. d

Page 61
1. c   2. a

This Award
Is Presented To

_____

for

★ Doing Your Best

★ Trying Hard

★ Not Giving Up

★ Making a
   Great Effort

64